W9-CYA-238

Vo-Vi Meditation

A Path to Self Healing of Mind and Body

⊙ Luong Si Hang ⊙

VoVi LED Publications

Published by
VoVi LED Publications
PO Box 5234
Oroville, CA 95966

**Edited and Translated
from the Vietnamese and Chinese by :**

Vo-Vi Practitioners

Copyright (c) 2001
by Luong Si Hang, VoVi Friendship Association of Northern
California, VoVi Association of Canada, VoVi Charitable Trust
of Australia

All Rights Reserved

website : http://www.vovi.org

ISBN 1-931245-00-2
First Edition 2001
Printed in HongKong

Contents

Foreword

Dear Friends,

In order to practice a Dharma of the Heart, we need to develop our spiritual heart and mind. However, we do not understand what the heart and mind are ? Where is their true position ? Therefore, we need this practical method of meditation to help us reach this necessary position. We should study the spiritual works of our predecessors, who truly want to guide us through their words of energy and self-awakening in numerous writings such as :

A) Taking part in Developing Your Heart and Mind,[1]

B) Vo-Vi Meditation : A path to self healing of mind and body.

We should carefully analyze each word in order to build an aura of serene energy and reach self-awakening.

Luong Si Hang

---

(1) Mr Luong's writings << Taking part in Developing Your Heart and Mind >> are available at the Vo-Vi website: http://www.vovi.org (English section) in the LED (Life Energy Development) weekly.

Alaska U.S.A., August,1998

AutoBiography

(excerpt from the videotape " The Practice of Vo-Vi Meditation "
realized in Boston Massachusetts in the year 1994)

My name is Hang Si Luong. I was born on November 13, 1923, in the province of Qui Nhon, Vietnam, I came from a family with many children. At that time, the society I lived in was deficient in every aspect. My mind was always preoccupied with how to grow up and help my family. As a boy, my school attendance was often interrupted by ill-health. I found that there was no opportunity for advancement, and I considered myself fortunate to have lived until the age of 30. However, I continued to live and all I saw was suffering on life's path. Everywhere I saw suffering. Everyone was suffering. Vietnam was a country full of suffering. When there were kings, only the kings were enjoying life, while the common people experienced hardship. If they were lucky, they would survive. Otherwise, they would die. And life went on.

I started different business ventures, and worked hard, but I was never successful, and became depressed. I then questioned myself: What is life? Why does mankind never reach happiness? Humans are born to live together, but they are competing against each other, and don't know how to love each other. My mind was then searching for God and the Buddhas. Who are God and the Buddhas? They are the supreme lightness of the upper spheres. Who is Buddha?

Buddha is a person who has freed himself from suffering and all karmic worries to return to his pure and serene nature.

I kept thinking about God and the Buddhas, the sacred scriptures, and the people who have dedicated their lives to spiritual perfection. When I listened to the Buddhist scriptures, I felt very attracted, but I didn't understand the reason. My mind was constantly involved in philosophical thinking. Then I noticed a change in my friend. His face was brighter and his eyes were livelier every day, and he talked in a very wise manner. I asked him how he had improved himself. He told me that he practiced meditation. At that time, I only enjoyed life's pleasures, and never paid attention to spiritual matters. So, I was discouraged when hearing about his spiritual inclination.

I didn't understand the meaning of spirituality. Then my friend introduced me to his Master, Mr. Do Thuan Hau, (also called Mr Tu, 1887-1966), [who lived] in Dakao, Saigon. When I met his Master, an elderly man, I was impressed by his very bright eyes and his intelligence. He spoke about God and the Buddhas, mountains, and waters. He spoke about many things that I could not understand. He spoke about my childhood. He said that my family liked to dress me up like a little girl, and everyone was loving me and helping me a lot.

I was surprised how he could know about my childhood. He must certainly be more pure and serene than I am. I wanted to know why this person knew so many things. In order to find out, I decided to bring the best people to test him.

So I brought two friends, a hypnotist, and a magician. We all came to visit him. My young friend told him: Please Sir, I will hypnotize you. Then he started hypnotizing Mr. Tu. After a while, the elderly man said: I am an old man. Please have pity of me. I didn't do anything wrong. Why do you want to hypnotize me? But my friend kept attempting to hypnotize him. After a while, my friend felt that his eyes were red, and he saw all heaven and earth in red. He became frightened . He pleaded for the elderly man to help him. Mr. Tu just smiled. He said: I already told you that I am old and worthless. You shouldn't hurt me. Do you understand what energy is now? Do you understand what fire is? The fire that you used to burn me didn't burn me, so it came back to you. Just sit down quietly, and everything will return to normal. When my friend came back to normal, he bowed in front of the Master, and asked to become his student. My other friend was a magician. He worked as a security guard for a movie theatre, and could be hit on the head without being harmed when he recited his magic words. Mr. Tu told him that a monk's spirit was walking around him. Did he want to eliminate the spirit, or keep living with him? My friend revealed that he had received a talisman in Cambodia to guard his life, and asked Mr. Tu to help him.

All three of us asked him to accept us as his students. Mr. Tu said that we were three dangerous pals. We had to follow an initiation ceremony and promised to dedicate our life to spiritual perfection.

My hypnotist friend made better progress than I did.

When he saw light and so on, he was rewarded by the Master. I was the one who was corrected the most. I was told that I was inadequate for spiritual practice, and that I should make great efforts. I just applied myself with dedication. I didn't speak a word. I just came to listen to his teachings, and kept practicing. I found that life was full of suffering. I practiced silently, day and night, all alone. My family was opposed to my spiritual practice, and everyone was rejecting me. Every day, I only ate one bowl of rice and a tomato to survive. I ate just enough to live and regain my original serenity. Day and night, I only practiced in a corner, and didn't even have a bed for sleeping. I began studying in 1957, and kept practicing until today.

I have encountered innumerable obstacles, both on the material and spiritual planes. But my mind is resolute to advance on the path of spiritual perfection. In order to find happiness, man has to revitalize his spiritual nature. The body does not bring happiness. It is subject to illness and can't resolve anything. Only the spiritual mind can resolve everything in a satisfactory manner. That is why I dedicate myself to spiritual perfection.

In Vietnam, many people came to my house to ask about spiritual matters. I answered all questions thoroughly. Since then, I am never free. Once abroad, I have never stopped helping the Vietnamese people with their sorrowful heart. When leaving the homeland, everyone's mind is burdened, and they would like to find more tranquility and happiness. For my part,

I have attained very good results from my daily practice. I would like to present the method that I am currently practicing to humanity.

Man is searching for his innate abilities, and his own inner mental order, but he can't understand himself. Every individual has potential in this universe. Our body is a microcosm composed of the five elements: metal, wood, water, fire, and earth with its five internal organs: heart, liver, stomach, lung, and kidneys, each having a color and light which provide the divine light and color. When we lose our serenity, we also lose the light in our inner consciousness. Only the practice of meditation will help us restore what we have lost.

We see clearly that life circumstances are our teacher. Despite all kinds of deprivation in this life, if we apply ourselves to attain serenity, and harmonize with everyone, we'll have everything. Today, the Vietnamese people have traveled around five continents to find what they have lost during many previous lives. People who are spiritually inclined will see clearly that they have lost their innate serenity.

In this materialistic society, the average person is attracted by material gains, and money is highly praised. But at last, only spirituality can release the sorrow hidden in his inner consciousness. Alas ! There are very few who understand the value of a serene soul.

Everyone carries his own worries without being able to resolve them. Serene people are spiritual people who have restored equilibrium to their body and mind, and whose energy can harmonize with the energy of the universe to produce pure and light vibrations. If we cannot harmonize with the pure and light vibrations of the universe of light, we do not have serenity. We are constantly torn by life's actions and reactions. Our sensuous desires will have no limit, and they will lead us nowhere.

I have practiced the Vo-Vi method until today, and I see that people are too agitated, and lack patience. Therefore, we must apply the Vo-Vi meditation which I have been practicing and with which I experienced good results in order to restore balance and serenity in our inner consciousness.

The Practice
of
Vo-Vi Meditation

Guidelines

- The best place in which to carry out the Vo-Vi Meditation is a quiet place, in the dark. For example, your bedroom, with door closed, lights turned off, and drapes/curtains closed.
- The best time during which to carry out the Vo-Vi Meditation is whenever it accomodates your lifestyle the best, when you feel the most comfortable, away from daily life stresses.
- The actual best hours to practice the meditation exercises are between 11 :00 pm and 1 :00 am, local time. Other hours are less desirable. Please remember to wait for 2 to 3 hours after a meal before practicing the Abdominal Breathing exercise.
- It is highly recommended that the Vo-Vi Meditation is carried out at the same place and at the same time every day, in order to create good habit and discipline, which, in turn, will help you focus and come to the state of meditative contemplation more easily in the future.
- During meditation, keep the spine straight and do not move back and forth. Do not lean against a chair and avoid direct contact with the ground. It is best to meditate on a carpet or a cushion. Sitting on a cushion will help to keep your backbone straight.
- The exercises of Concentration of Energy and Contemplative Meditation are done in the sitting position, facing Southward.

- At the start of each practice session, mentally remember your purpose and direction. Please see the section entitled " Making a Spiritual Commitment " on page 8
- During the practice session, if the mind starts getting cluttered with life's daily worries, mentally repeat the Six Vibratory Sounds (Nam Mo A Di Da Phat) (nahm moh ah yee da fut) in order to release these worries and focus again on your practice. Please see the section entitled " Invoking the mantra of Nam Mo A Di Da Phat " on page 20 for further information.

During the entire practice session, constantly keep the following positions :

1. The tongue : In a natural and relaxed position, let the tip of your tongue lightly touch the line between your uppper gum and your front teeth.
2. Incisors against incisors: Front teeth slightly touching together.
3. The mouth : In a natural and relaxed position, keep your mouth closed.
4. The eyes : In a natural and relaxed position, keep your eyes closed and focus forward from the center point between your eyebrows.

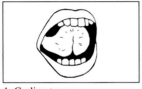

1. Curling tongue

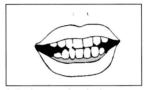

2. Incisors againts incisors

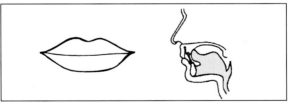

3. Mouth closed in a natural position with curling tongue and upper and lower teeth touching.

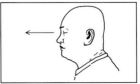

4. Eyes closed and focused on the center point between the eyebrows

THE SITTING POSITION

Sit on a cushion on top of a carpet to avoid direct contact with the ground and keep a straight spine. Fold your legs such that the knees touch the carpet to establish a good balance and keep a straight backbone.

1. Lotus position : Fold the legs with soles of both feet facing upward.

2. Half-lotus position : Fold the legs with sole of one foot facing upward.

3. Crossed leg position : Fold the legs naturally in the crossed leg position.

4. Sitting on a chair (only for those who cannot sit in the crossed leg position) :
   Keep the spine straight, and do not lean on the back of the chair. Avoid direct contact with the ground by keeping your shoes on or, if barefooted, with the feet fully touching each other, and the soles laying flat on the carpet or a piece of wood.

BASIC TECHNIQUES DURING THE FIRST SIX MONTHS

For the first six months, you should practice the following three exercises with care and diligence :

1. **Concentration of Energy**
2. **Abdominal Breathing**
3. **Invoking the mantra of Nam Mo A Di Da Phat**

These exercises aim at helping you gradually prepare yourself to fully and correctly carry out the actual Vo-Vi Meditation Practice. The exercise of Concentration of Spiritual Energy helps relieve stress and restore balance to the brain and nervous system. The exercise of Lying Down Abdominal Breathing purifies and regulates the intestinal system. By cleansing the toxins from the body, you will be able to concentrate the spiritual energy on the top of your head. Once you understand the principle of Nam Mo A Di Da Phat through the exercise of silent invocation, you will be able to continue with the advanced practice of the exercises of Concentrating Your Spiritual Energy, Continuous Breathing in Cycles, and Meditative Contemplation in the future.

MAKING A SPIRITUAL COMMITMENT

The practice session starts with making a spiritual commitment.

- Sitting down, facing Southward, with back bone straight and legs folded in one of the positions mentioned previously.
- In a natural and relaxed position, let the tip of your tongue lightly touch the line between your upper gum and your front teeth. Keep the mouth closed. In a natural and relaxed position, keep your eyes closed, and focus forward from the center point between your eyebrows.
- Keep the palm of your hands fully touching each other, in prayer position, at chest level.

- **Focusing your mind at the top of your head, mentally repeat the following mantras :**

> Nam Mo A Di Da Phat (3 times)
> [nahm moh ah yee dah fut]

Repeat **2 times** :

- Nam Mo Tay Phuong Cuc Lac The Gioi Quan The Am Bo Tat
[nahm moh taay phu-ung kuk lakh teh zuh/oy kwan teh ahm boh taht]
(Pure Divine Energy of Compassion)

- Nam Mo Long Hoa Giao Chu Di Lac
[nahm mo laumng hua zao chuu zi lakh]
(Pure Divine Energy of Serenity)

- I am (use your name) Please accept my sincere promise to pursue the
 spiritual path to reach enlightenment and liberation of my soul.

Next mentally repeat the following phrases **1 time** :
- From now on, I will strive to :
- Quy y Phat [Kwi ee fut] (Return to my true nature of serenity)
- Quy y Phap [Kwi ee fap] (Return to my true nature of spiritual energy)
- Quy y Tang [Kwi ee tang] (Return to my true nature of my duties towards
 my fellow beings, Heaven and Earth)
- Nam Mo A Di Da Phat
- May Peace be with all creatures

- Then bow 3 times with your hands. Keep your spine straight,
 not bowing.

CONCENTRATION OF SPIRITUAL ENERGY

This exercises helps relieve stress and restore balance to the brain and nervous system.

After the Spiritual Commitment, continue with the exercise of **Concentration of Spiritual Energy.**

During this exercise, constantly keep the following position : Sitting down, Facing Southward, With legs folded in one of the positions mentioned previously, The backbone straight, The tip of the tongue lightly touching the line between your gum and your front teeth ; The mouth closed. The eyes closed, looking straight ahead of you from the center point between the eyebrows, and breathing normally.

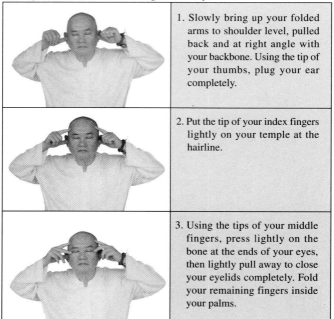

	1. Slowly bring up your folded arms to shoulder level, pulled back and at right angle with your backbone. Using the tip of your thumbs, plug your ear completely.
	2. Put the tip of your index fingers lightly on your temple at the hairline.
	3. Using the tips of your middle fingers, press lightly on the bone at the ends of your eyes, then lightly pull away to close your eyelids completely. Fold your remaining fingers inside your palms.

Hold this position for at least five minutes to a maximum of fifteen minutes.

Notes :

In order to correctly identify the location at the temple area where your forefingers should press down at the hairline, lightly bite your jaws together. You will feel a point at the hairline where the temple muscle slightly moves as your jaws bite down ; that point is the correct point to press down with the tip of your forefingers.

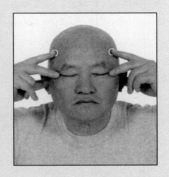

While doing this exercise, if your mind should start getting cluttered with thoughts and worries, practice the silent invocation of the mantra Nam Mo A Di Da Phat to gradually move away from these and focus again on the exercise.

THE LYING DOWN ABDOMINAL BREATHING

This exercise purifies the body and regulates the function of the intestinal system.

After the Spiritual Commitment and the Concentration of Spiritual Energy, you can continue with the Lying Down Abdominal Breathing exercise.

During this exercise, you breathe through your abdomen and mentally focus on your navel at the same time. You may practice this method any time your stomach is not full, or 2 to 3 hours after a meal. You may practice it after the exercise of concentration of spiritual energy, or do it separately at any time during the day.

The following position should be kept during the entire exercise :
• Lay down on your back on a firm flat surface, preferably in a quiet location where you will not be disturbed for the entire length of the exercise. Keep your arms and legs fully extended out, limp and relaxed. Tell yourself to forget about your body.
• Close your mouth, let the tip of your tongue lightly touch the line between your upper gum and your front teeth.
• Close your eyes, look straight ahead from the center point between your eyebrows, and focus your attention at your navel. Keep this mental focus at the navel for the entire length of the exercise.

- Start by exhaling through your nose and gradually flatten your abdomen as much as possible. Slowly inhale to inflate the abdomen without holding your breath. Slowly exhale until the abdomen is completely flattened. After a complete inhalation and exhalation, mentally count " One " breath.

- Continue inhaling and exhaling the next breath and count " 2 ". Don't hold your breath, breathe evenly, and count " 3 ". Continue, counting 4, 5, 6, 7, 8, 9, 10, 11 up to 12. This completes one cycle.

- Rest for a few seconds, and begin a new cycle. With each new cycle, you will be dropping a number.   Slowly exhale, empty your abdomen, and start again with 1. Continue breathing and count only up to 11. The next time count only up to 10, then 9, and so on. 1 to 8... 1 to 7... 1 to 6 ... 1 to 5 ... 1 to 4... 1 to 3... 1 to 2... and finally, just " 1 ". Having counted the last breath ends the entire Lying Down Abdominal Breathing.

- The total number of breaths should be 78 or twelve cycles. Your breathing must be smooth and rhythmic. If you go too fast, you will get less results. If you go too slowly, it is easy to fall asleep.

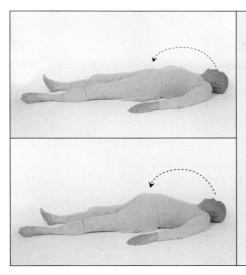

Start by slowly exhaling, gradually flattening out your abdomen, then, start to inhale slowly to gradually fill up the navel and the abdomen. Remember to mentally look forward from the center point between your eyebrows and focus your attention at the navel during the whole exercise.

At the beginning, if you find it difficult to breathe with the abdomen, lay a small pillow on top of your abdomen to help you learn to focus on the navel during inhalation and exhalation.

POST-MEDITATION MASSAGE

After the exercise of Concentration of Energy or after the Contemplative Meditation, do the following massage to draw energy back to your body :

1.Rub your hands together to warm them (while rubbing your hands, the fingers must point upward).	
2. Cover your nose with your palms, and rub your face.	
3. Slowly raise both hands to your head.	
4. Cover your head with your palms to draw energy back to your body.	

5. Slide your hands down along the side of your head.	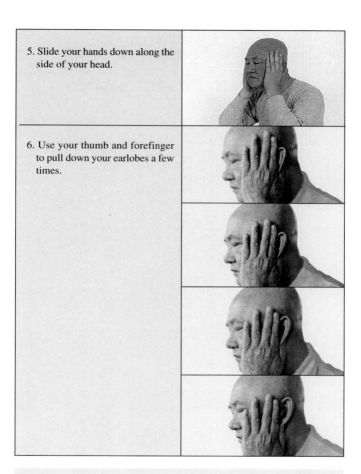
6. Use your thumb and forefinger to pull down your earlobes a few times.	

- Repeat the movements from Picture 2 to Picture 6 two times.
- You should rub your face like this three times.

7. Rub your hands together to warm them.

8. Massage your arms to regulate the blood circulation from shoulder down to wrist, then acupress the outside ends of your palms. Do this 3 times on each arm.

9. Again, rub your hands together to warm them.

10. Massage your legs from thighs down to feet with your palms. Do this 3 times on each leg.

11. Finally, hold the soles of your feet together with your hands, then rub them together 50 times.

You should do all these movements for a complete massage after the Concentration of Spiritual Energy for beginners or after meditation for advanced practitioners.

NOTES

• If your legs or feet are numb from meditating in the sitting position, press the end of the big toe nail and bend the toe down. At the same time, use your thumb and fingers to press on the two acupoints on your knee to slowly release the numbness (see picture).

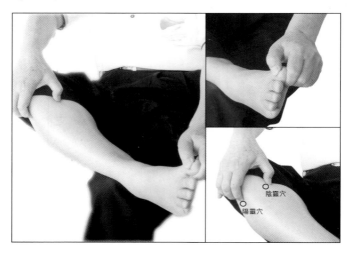

• If your legs or feet are numb, you should follow the method above to release the numbness before doing the movement in Picture 11, i.e., before rubbing the soles of your feet together 50 times.

INVOKING THE MANTRA OF NAM MO A DI DA PHAT

- Invoke the mantra silently, keeping your mouth closed, incisors against incisors, and tongue curled up to the upper gum.
- Invoking this mantra with eyes and mouth closed helps you to mentally close the door to earthly matters and open the gate of Heaven.
- You can practice this invocation at any time. With time, the flow of your saliva will increase. If needed, slowly turn your head toward your left to swallow it. Gradually, your saliva will sweeten as it gains potent therapeutic effect, helping to protect your body from ailments.
- Use your mind to slowly and correctly sound out each of the Six Words, especially focusing on the resonance at the end of each word (i.e., Nah...ummmm). These resonating sounds will move the energy vibrations into the corresponding energy centers of your physical body.

Curl your tongue up, teeth to teeth, mouth and eyes closed, and invoke each word in your mind :

- **NAM** (Nah...ummm) : When you invoke " Nam ", watch for the resonance within your physical body, creating vibrations merging at the midpoint between your eyebrows. Vibrations emitted by the final -ummm sound of the Word NAM impact the energy center located at the middle point between the eyebrows. (Pict. 1)

- **MO** (Mohhhhh): When you invoke " Mo ", watch for the internal resonance. Vibrations emitted by the final -ohhh sound of the Word MO impact the energy center located at the top of your head. (Pict. 2)

- **A** (Ahhh): When you invoke " A ", vibrations emitted by the final -ahhh- sound of the Word A impact the energy center located at the midpoint between your kidneys. (Pict. 3)

- **DI** (Yeee or Zeee) : When you invoke " Di ", vibrations emitted by the final --Yeee- sound of the Word DI impact the energy center located at the middle of your chest area. (Pict. 4)

- **DA** (Dahhhh) : Vibrations emitted by the final -ahhh- sound of the Word DA impact energy centers at all the pores on the surface of your skin, emitting peaceful light (Pict. 5)

- **PHAT** (Fut) : When you invoke " Phat ", watch for the echoes, and vibrations that merge at the area of your navel. (Pict. 6)

NAM

MO

A

DI

DA

PHAT

Concentrate and use your mind to invoke the mantra Nam Mo A Di Da Phat while placing the resonance of each word onto the corresponding energy center of your body. You may practice for the first six months or until you can start feeling the flow of energy pulling on the top of your head. At that time, you will only need to focus at the center top of your head while practicing the silent invocation of Nam Mo A Di Da Phat. When you clearly understand the principle of the six vibratory sounds Nam Mo A Di Da Phat, you will no longer be subject to superstition.

Explanatory Notes

Meaning of the Mantras during Spiritual Commitment

- **Nam Mo A Di Da Phat** [nahm moh ah yee da fut] : Nam is fire. Mo is air. A is water. Di is expansion. Da is emanation of light and color. Phat is serenity of mind and body. Everything on this earth, from a blade of grass to the human body, resides within this principle.
- The energy of **Quan The Am Bo Tat** [kwan teh ahm boh taht) or Kwan Yin Bodhisattva is perfect pureness that shines down to the earthly world. Invoking <<Quan The Am Bo Tat>> helps the meditation practitioner to awaken his consciousness and develop his soul.
- The energy of **Long Hoa Giao Chu Di Lac** [nahm moh laumng hua zao chuu yee lakh] or the Maitreya Buddha is basically inner joy, great happiness, and serenity within, which result from good deeds. Invoking <<Long Hoa Giao Chu Di Lac>> helps to awaken the soul so that it can return to its essential quietness in order to guide all conscious beings.
- **Quy Y Phat** (Return to my true nature of serenity) means to release the karma of heart, to return to purity and lightness, to return to our Buddha-nature.
- **Quy Y Phap** (Return to my true nature of spiritual energy) means to practice the dharma correctly. A righteous Dharma releases the impure energy and preserves the pure energy.
- **Quy Y Tang** means to return to my true nature, to be aware of my true soul and fulfill my duties towards my fellow beings, Heaven and Earth.

CONCENTRATION OF SPIRITUAL ENERGY

The exercise of concentrating spiritual energy stabilizes the energy in our brains and nervous system which we have disrupted by turning outward and entangling ourselves into earthly matters. Now we practice this exercise to concentrate our spiritual energy and redirect it towards the true consciousness ; we will be able to release the karma of the heart, and slowly reduce our agitation and attraction to external matters day after day.

During the practice of concentration of energy, whenever our mind drifts towards worldly affairs, we should refocus our thoughts on the silent invocation of the mantra Nam Mo A Di Da Phat. After a while, we will dissipate all worries about earthly matters.

During the whole exercise, we should concentrate at the middle point between the eyebrows. We should always focus forward at this center point. Human character likes to deviate. This exercise will help to rectify a human's character so that he will become a righteous person. Those who practice correctly will learn to keep their promises faithfully. Parents give birth to their child, but they cannot rectify their child's character. Only when the child corrects himself, will he be able to attain peace and harmony.

Profane people like to ponder upon things and weaken their mind in this manner without knowing how to concentrate their energy to revitalize their brain to make it stronger, purer, and lighter each day.

No religion on earth has yet practiced this concentration of energy to develop the energy center on the top of the head and let the vibrations evolve into infinity.

When you start the exercise by raising your elbows level with your shoulders, you activate the nerves linked to all five inner organs (heart, liver, stomach, lungs, and kidneys). This causes you to perspire. When putting your thumbs in your ears to close them - you may hear a lot of buzzing sounds in your head, which means that you still have a hot temper. In time, you will not hear them anymore and will start to feel serene.

While practicing the concentration of spiritual energy, you may notice various bodily reactions, such as perspiring, eyes filling with tears, running nose, or itching. There should be no worry since these are good signs of purification. After finishing the exercise, just wipe off the perspiration. Slowly, after a period of practice, you will feel stronger and healthier. Bodily reactions like perspiring will occur more rarely and stop completely.

During daily activities, we spend a lot of our energy to earn a living, thus we experience mental stress that harms our nervous system. So after work, we can do this exercise at home to strengthen the energy frequency of our mind and recuperate the energy lost through the day.

When using the thumbs to close your ears, you are converging the energy to the head and concentrating it on the middle point between your eyebrows. Your forefingers and middle fingers above your temples and at the outside ends of the eyes are also transmitting the energy to the middle point between your eyebrows. After practicing this exercise for a period of time, you will feel some heaviness at this energy center -- like a spinning wheel. When you are able to concentrate your energy, light will project out from the middle point between the eyebrows. Your energy will proceed to the correct middle path and lead you directly to the universal central source of vital energy. You mind will then become more and more at ease.

For those who have an amputated arm or fingers, you can use a cotton ball to close your ear instead of using your finger. For those who have an amputated leg, you do not need to sit cross-legged, but you should sit with a straight back, without leaning on the chair.

While practicing this exercise, avoid moving your body or balancing your head. Sit with a straight back, and keep a straight head, without nodding down while focusing forward at the middle point between the eyebrows.

It is recommended that beginners practice this exercise for at least six months to strengthen the mind. We have absorbed too much impurity due to agitation. Therefore, we have to first correct and purify our mind. Whenever you have any spare time, you may practice this concentration of spiritual energy to calm yourself and eliminate unnecessary stress.

Abdominal Breathing
(Continuous breathing in cycles in the lying position)

The exercise of abdominal breathing helps to increase our patience and re-establish our clarity of mind. Beginners may have difficulty in practicing this exercise at first, but it is an important one. They should practice it to gradually regulate their breathing before starting to meditate in the sitting position.

Why do we breathe in ? To cleanse our intestinal system and let it function in a light and orderly manner. The intestine provides energy to the brain ; therefore, we must care for both our brain and intestine. Our astral body will only become lighter when both our brain and intestine function harmoniously.

Why do you have to think of " filling up " your navel ? By " filling up " your navel, you have instantly focused on your kidneys, because there is a direct relationship between your navel and kidneys. When you fill your navel by inhaling, you have created a pressure against your kidneys at your back. Thus, the exhaling and inhaling will form one cycle of continuous breath. Then do the second cycle of breath continuously to build a pressure force to expel the impure energy of your kidneys and organs out through the way of excretion. Do continuously one cycle to twelve cycles of abdominal breathing. Those gentle breath cycles will create a pressure on your kidneys, leading to the expulsion of impure energy out through your waste and perspiration. It will also unblock part of the impure energy of your spine.

During the exercise of abdominal breathing, when you look at your navel, you will eventually focus on your astral body. This connection will assist you in the union of your soul and astral body, once the order of your body reaches its point of equilibrium. To attain lightness, we must be aware of both our soul and astral body. To be light means to be healthy and free of diseases.

After the Adbominal Breathing, we will enjoy a very sound sleep. It is best to practice this exercise 2 to 3 times a day. We will equally care for our brain and our intestine. We will also stabilize our liver, and provide a good blood circulation throughout our body.

Beginners, especially athletes who are used to breathing with their chest, probably will experience difficulty breathing with their abdomen. However, they should make an effort and be determined to achieve !

Men who are pleasure lovers will certainly weaken their vital energy and shorten their breath. Women who give birth to many children will experience the same ; their vital energy will be weakened too. In those cases, if you adopt this abdominal breathing, you will gradually recuperate the lost energy and will become stronger and conscious of many things. You will also prevent incurable diseases such as paralysis, liver and heart ailments.

Our microcosm contains the elements of water, fire, wind, and earth. Our heart, liver, stomach, lungs, and kidneys, as well as our arms, legs, and skin also belong to the original principle of these four elements. If we don't use these four elements, how can we purify our microcosm ? What is more real than using the pure vital breath of the cosmic universe to cleanse ourselves and to purify the organs of this microcosm ?

In our organism, the five elements : metal, wood, water, fire, and earth also contain impure energy within. We must release this impure energy to re-establish our spontaneous nature. Only when we fully harmonize with nature will our body become peaceful and serene, and our mind will gain greater wisdom and clarity.

INVOKING THE MANTRA OF
NAM MO A DI DA PHAT

We must understand the original principle of NAM MO A DI DA PHAT when invoking this mantra. Nam is fire, Mo is air, A is water, Di is expansion, Da is emanation of light and color, and Phat is inspiration. Everything on this earth can be condensed into this principle, from a blade of grass to the human body. All belong to the four elements : water, fire, wind, and earth.

When we curl our tongue up to our upper gum, teeth against teeth, mouth closed, and use our mind to invoke the mantra of Nam Mo A Di Da Phat, we let the energy vibrations of the original principle of Nam Mo A Di Da Phat circulate throughout our body. Only when the energy vibrations move to the corresponding energy centers of the body, will the soul become light and form an aura like the Buddha A DI DA. He only practiced the silent invocation of the mantra Nam Mo A Di Da Phat for his spiritual training, but He could travel everywhere.

• NAM truly represents the South Gate of Heaven and the South Binh Dinh Fire. The energy flow on each side of your forehead will build up at the middle point between your eyebrows. These two energies will then connect and spark brightly. Why do we invoke the word " NAM " ? Nam enables the concentration of energy at the middle point between the eyebrows, and the harmonization with the South direction of Heaven and Earth. When fire generates fire, energy shines faster and will help the soul to attain higher levels.

• MO shows the invisible things. When we close our eyes, we can view the scenery from above.

• A Nham Qui (ah neyammm qui) gathers in the kidneys. Water and energy come together in the spiritual renal water. When the kidneys don't function well, you cannot sleep, but when water and energy connect, you feel better and sleep well.

• DI preserves the 3 precious energies : the seminal essence of life, the vital breath energy, and spiritual energy. These three energies come together to progress upward and stabilize you.

• DA is an aura, a golden color that covers everything. When we are serene, a spiritual energy in the form of a golden aura radiates over our entire body and protects it.

• PHAT is recognizing the serenity inside ourselves. We must admit our problems so as to repent. We must repent to permit progress toward enlightenment.

When we admit our problems, we should remember to practice regularly the invocation of the mantra at the six corresponding chakras during the day whenever we have some leisure time. We will no longer follow superstititous rites and beliefs, and we will no longer pray for favors vainly. On this earth, everyone wants the help of others, but they refuse to develop themselves. Therefore, they keep following a spiritual practice without seeing Buddha. We must develop ourselves through our own efforts in order to attain higher levels. We will then meet Buddha, we will arrive at the sphere of lightness and purity, and we will be able to live forever in peace and happiness at this shore of enlightenment.

Therefore, we must build our own serenity and purity. We must develop our enlightened consciousness. Then we will slowly gather our aura. A Vo-Vi practitioner who understands the principle of Nam Mo A Di Da Phat with a sincere heart, will be able to see light after closing his eyes for a while, instead of feeling anger and frustration like in the past...

As a Vo-Vi practitioner, you should remember the principle of Nam Mo A Di Da Phat. At the beginning, you practice the silent invocation of the mantra Nam Mo A Di Da Phat. With time, you will just remember the mantra, and understand its principle. When you are able to focus energy on the top of your head, you will always feel the pull of energy at this central point. At that time, you will always remember Nam Mo A Di Da Phat.

It is more difficult to completely harmonize with the principle of Nam Mo A Di Da Phat than to invoke it mentally. Only when you are light and pure, will you constantly remember the mantra Nam Mo A Di Da Phat.

When you constantly remember the mantra Nam Mo A Di Da Phat, you will live within the principle of Nam Mo A Di Da Phat, and you will be able to bring peace and happiness to all beings in all domains in the future.

Completion of this book was made possible by the loving support of many Vo-Vi practitioners.

To learn more about the advanced Vo Vi technique and other Vo Vi literature, please visit the website:

http://www.vovi.org

To make a donation for book printing, please contact:

USA
VoVi Friendship Association of Northern California
P.O Box 18304
San Jose, CA 95158, USA

Canada
VoVi Association of Canada
2922 Jolicoeur
Montreal, Quebec, H4E1Z3
Canada

Australia
VoVi Charitable Trust
P.O. Box 197
Sunshine, Victoria 3020
Australia

Printed for Free Distribution/Not for Sale

VoVi LED Publications